7 STEPS *to* CREATING *an* HEIR-TIGHT WILL

Essential Tips to Simplify Complex Situations & Ensure Your Will Works

RACHAEL RODGERS

Heir Tight Wills & Estate Planning Ltd.

90-Day Books

British Library Cataloguing in Publication Data.

A catalogue record for this book is available from the British Library.

Paperback Edition   ISBN 978-1-908101-65-5

Digital Edition   ISBN 978-1-908101-66-2

V01

CONTENTS

ACKNOWLEDGMENTS

ACKNOWLEDGMENTS

To my family and friends over the years who encouraged me to start my own business. You were right!

To my Clients who have given me the opportunity to flourish in a field that is my passion, and left me basking in the satisfaction that I have always left them in a better situation than I found them in!

To Steve Wilkes of Silver Lining Estate Planning Ltd, my first mentor in the field of Wills and estate planning, who gave far more than he received, and reinforced my belief that to succeed in business you need little more than Professionalism, Credibility, Integrity and Transparency.

To my numerous business networking contacts, who gave me the power to speak, and the ability to practice my presentations in a fun, friendly and pressure-free environment.

To my Professional Introducers – financial advisors, accountants and solicitors, whose trust and faith in both me and my services, has provided me with a successful business doing something I love. They have also been the inspiration for me to write this book - to help their clients, and many potential others around the country, to protect the ones they love, and make sure their assets go where they want them to.

To Jonathan Jay, Daniel Priestley, Lee Gilbert, Peter Thomson and Kevin Bermingham - the people I have learned from, and consider to be, some of the best business mentors around. They have helped me over the last few years to take my business to where it is now, and without them I would never have written this book!

To Caroline Coleman, Wes Mason, Jon Alexander, Julia Russell and Ann & Bruce Rodgers - the people who have very rigorously critiqued this book, from every angle, and provided some really constructive feedback and invaluable input.

To Andrew Davies, owner of Cricket Ltd - a client who kindly provided a testimonial for the cover of my book.

Thank you all!

INTRODUCTION

INTRODUCTION

If you don't have a Will, don't worry; the Government has one for you!

Unfortunately it won't be one you want, and it's very unlikely to do what you want or need it to do.

Nearly 70% of people in the UK die without a Will. And of those that have Wills, some 28% are found to have major flaws that totally change the way assets are distributed.

Nearly seventy percent of people in the UK die without a Will. And of those that have Wills, some twenty-eight percent are found to have major flaws that totally change the way assets are distributed.

There are so many things you need to be aware of in order to make sure your family - and your business - are secure after you're gone, just getting started can be intimidating.

Dying without a Will, or without a valid Will, is called dying *Intestate*, for which the Government has a set of rules that govern how your estate will be distributed – *the Rules of Intestacy* - and they rarely reflect what you would actually want to happen. Everybody over the age of eighteen, who has children or their own assets, should have a Will. It's as simple as that.

Unfortunately, throughout my years of experience as a specialist Will Writer and Estate Planner, I've seen the effects of far too many people being unprepared; dying unexpectedly without having made (or updated) their Will, and leaving their loved ones to pick up the pieces.

For example, I often meet people who have been through two, three or even more marriages, very often with children from more than one relationship. They've not made a Will because they see their situation as so complicated they wouldn't know where to start. They need professional advice; to ensure they take into account all the members of their various families they want to provide for, or who may have a legal claim for part of their estate after their death, otherwise their latest family are likely to get a very nasty shock.

For many people the situation can indeed be very complex – not only those who need to take into account the needs of *blended families*, but also those who have extensive assets making them liable to a substantial tax liability on death, and those who run their own company and need to consider business succession planning. Many people need to provide for beneficiaries who would not be capable of managing their own affairs. Or they have children with issues of their own (such as a pending divorce or bankruptcy), for whom it may not be advisable to inherit outright. And the list goes on.

It is for these people that I have written this book – in plain English, not legal jargon! I've collected together the most essential tips I've been passing on over many years of assisting business owners, senior executives, and people with extensive estates and complex family situations. You'll find out exactly what you need to take into account; to ensure both your personal and business affairs are left in order after you're gone, and to avoid the most common perils and pitfalls people unwittingly fall foul of when making their Wills.

The book is split into seven easy-to-understand steps. They explain the key issues, their consequences, the relevant provisions you can put in place to protect the ones you love, and ensure your assets go where you want them to. Most importantly, the book highlights the importance of using a qualified, specialist advisor to draft your documents. Because your Will is not only one of the most important documents you'll ever write, it's also the largest cheque you'll ever write – it disposes of all your assets!

> *Your Will is not only one of the most important documents you'll ever write, it's also the largest cheque you'll ever write - it disposes of all your assets!*

Knowledge is the key to success, because you don't know what you don't know! Everyone's situation and requirements are different, and can change substantially and regularly throughout their lives. Whether you're single, married/civil partners*, separated, divorced, remarried, co-habiting, have children, own assets or run a business – it is essential to have a relevant, valid, up-to-date Will.

One of the first steps in making a Will involves deciding who to appoint to various roles; to sort out your affairs after you're gone and look after your young children. This book will guide you through the selection process; to ensure you pick the right people. It will also help you decide *what, when and how* to provide for your chosen beneficiaries, and how best to protect your estate from unwanted third parties – essentially helping you to control your assets from beyond the grave.

It will help you to (legally!) avoid leaving the Government a legacy in your Will by paying unnecessary amounts of *Inheritance Tax* on your death (the death tax); and show you what other provisions you can make in your lifetime to ease the tax burden. Equally importantly, it covers the issues that arise when dealing with foreign assets, and foreign beneficiaries.

And then there are the provisions required to ensure the effective continuity of your business. Without making proper provision during your lifetime, a business partnership would fail on the death of one of the partners. For a limited company the situation could be equally dire – after all, if one of your fellow business owners died, would you want their spouse or children to take over?

Having explained the provisions you can put in place to take care of your affairs after your death, I would only be doing half a job if I didn't also help prepare you for losing mental capacity before you die - which could happen to anyone at any time. Step 6 covers *Powers of Attorney*, which should be a very serious consideration for every adult. Because if you don't appoint people to manage your affairs; your family will suffer years of intrusion and expense, in having to deal with the Government appointed *Court of Protection*, to get permission for ALL decisions involving your finances and welfare!

I imagine you already have some idea of how essential it is to put robust provision in place for the people you leave behind; or you wouldn't be reading this book! I've heard dreadful stories far too often, about families left in terrible situations because of the lack of a valid Will, or by inadequate lifetime planning, and you probably know of people who have suffered a similar fate.

Please read this book to prepare yourself.   Having your own professionally-drafted Will, with the relevant supporting provisions, will protect your loved ones and preserve your assets.

Rachael

Rachael Rodgers - Aff STEP, MIPW, MSWW
Specialist Will Writer and Estate Planner

* Throughout this book - unless otherwise indicated - all references to *marriage* or *spouse* also include civil partners, as they have the same legal rights as married couples under most circumstances.

HTW
HEIR TIGHT WILLS

STEP 1: WHO TO APPOINT AS EXECUTORS AND TRUSTEES

STEP 1: WHO TO APPOINT AS EXECUTORS AND TRUSTEES

WHY YOU NEED THEM

The purpose of your Will is to ensure your *estate* (everything you own) passes as you want it to after your death. When you die, any assets in your sole name are frozen until *probate* is completed. Probate is the process of proving your Will is valid and valuing your assets. And your *Executors* are the people responsible for going to court to obtain the *Grant of Probate*. The grant allows the ownership of your assets to be transferred from your estate to your executors, so they can then carry out the terms of your Will.

Typically your executors would also act as trustees if required under your Will. The trustees are the people you appoint to look after any assets you don't want to go directly to a beneficiary. For example, they will take care of money left to your young children, until they are old enough to inherit in their own right - normally between the ages of eighteen and twenty-five - depending on your wishes.

This money (the Trust Fund) will be held *in Trust*. This simply means it has been left with conditions, which are specified in your Will. A Trust lets you keep some control of your assets even after you die. For example, in protecting assets from unwanted third parties; such as the remarriage or care fees of your surviving spouse, or your child's pending divorce settlement.

Most estates will need to go through probate. It's not a question of whether you had a Will, but the type of assets you own, which determine if a Grant of Probate is required. For example, if you held £50,000 in a bank account, the bank would require sight of the grant before releasing your money to your executors. Likewise, if you owned stocks and shares, the Registrar would need to see the grant before transferring the shares into the names of your executors or beneficiaries. And, if your home is owned in your sole name, a grant will be necessary before it can be sold, or ownership transferred.

On the other hand, you may own your home jointly with someone (e.g. a surviving spouse) as *joint tenants* (meaning you each effectively own 100% of the property), as opposed to *tenants in common* (where you each own a share, totalling 100%, e.g. 50:50). As *joint tenants*, the property will pass to the other 100% joint-owner simply by them surviving you, with no grant required. Whereas, as *tenants in common*, your share will pass under the terms of your Will; and will require a grant.

If your savings with any one institution are relatively small (typically under £15,000), and there is no property to be transferred or shares to be sold, you may be in luck and not need a grant. However, it only needs the holder of one asset (e.g. your bank) to insist on seeing a grant, and the whole estate will become involved in the probate process.

THEIR ROLES AND RESPONSIBILITIES

Being an executor is a significant role, with both legal and financial responsibilities. If they make an error or omission that comes to light many years later, they may be held financially liable at that time, and they can be fined if they act inappropriately. The role includes:

Identifying and correctly valuing ALL the assets and debts / liabilities in your estate

To find out what you are worth at the time of your death, the executors have to write to everyone you have assets with, along with everyone you trade with and might owe money to. They are responsible for all the assets in your estate until such time as they are actually passed to the beneficiaries, or into a Trust. With regards to a solely owned property, one of the executor's first responsibilities is to change the locks to prevent your beneficiaries going in and picking the place clean.

You can greatly aid the *identification* part of the executor's role during your lifetime; by keeping an up to date record for them, listing all your relevant accounts, investments, property, etc. In addition, listing anyone you owe money to; such as mortgage or finance companies, and any Direct Debits or Standing Orders in force, e.g. for telecoms and utilities, memberships, subscriptions, etc.

Completing income tax and inheritance tax returns

Executors are responsible for arranging for the payment of outstanding tax bills. They must ensure any *Inheritance Tax* (the death tax) due on your estate is paid. This must be paid before they can receive the Grant of Probate. If there are insufficient funds in your estate to pay the tax - or there is no Life Assurance to meet the bill - the executors may be forced to take out a bank loan; at the cost of the estate, and ultimately your beneficiaries.

Applying for the *Grant of Probate*, and then gathering in your assets

The executors will value the assets and debts in the estate, complete the tax returns, submit the probate forms, and pay any tax due. All being well, they will be issued with the grant. The executors then need to collect in all your assets. This involves writing again to anyone who holds your assets; then closing your accounts, selling your shares and selling or transferring your property, etc.

Using the assets to settle the estate costs and your debts

Many people assume that debt will be written off on the death of the borrower. This is not generally the case, and the situation for your executors can become very difficult when the debt is unexpected; or no provision for its repayment has been made.

Once the executors have collected in any money or property you owned, they must pay any unpaid debts before any of your beneficiaries receive anything. If there are not enough assets to cover all the debts, bills will need to be paid in order of priority. Mortgages are paid first; then rent dues, followed by water bills, council tax, other utilities, loans, credit cards, and then anyone else, e.g. payment of your funeral costs. The beneficiaries of your Will only receive their dues when, or if, all your accumulated debt has been repaid.

No one else has to pay for the debts unless they are already liable under the terms of the original agreement; such as a mortgage or loan in joint names, or if they have signed as a guarantor. For example, if the money left in your estate is not sufficient to cover the outstanding debt and your surviving spouse jointly owns your property, then they may have to sell it to meet your creditors' demands.

It is also the executor's responsibility to retrieve money owed to you, especially when there is a written agreement in place. If, however, you and the borrower had agreed a loan on a casual basis, the debt may be irrecoverable as it could be impossible to prove. If it is your intention to release a borrower (e.g. one of your children) from repaying a loan or debt on your death - or to have it considered as an advancement of their inheritance - then this needs to be detailed in your Will.

Paying out the legacies specified in your Will

After all your debts, liabilities and estate administration expenses have been met, the executors can finally distribute the gifts, legacies and residual estate according to the terms of your Will.

Setting up a Trust Fund

Your Will may contain a Trust, e.g. for your young children. If so, your trustees will take over managing the Trust once your executors have sold your assets, set up the Trust bank account, and transferred the relevant funds into it.

A trustee's role is a very responsible one, and they are accountable for their decisions and actions. They act on behalf of the Trust, to manage and distribute assets for the exclusive benefit of the named Trust beneficiaries. They are subject to the Trust instructions in your Will, which detail the powers the trustees have (and don't have), and various applicable laws and regulations. The role includes planning, meetings with co-trustees, decision making, correspondence and recordkeeping, preparing accounts, and paying relevant taxes to the Government (Her Majesty's Revenue and Customs, HMRC).

IMPORTANT SELECTION CRITERIA

Lay person or professional

The choice of executors and trustees is a very personal one. You are free to choose any individual/s, professional company, or a mixture of both to undertake the role, and all executors have equal authority. If appointing a professional firm, consider how long they might be in existence, and if you would still want them to act if you had moved out of the area.

You should discuss the appointment with your intended executors and trustees to ensure they are prepared to act, and understand their responsibilities. Nobody appointed in a Will is committed to the role; effectively they are just given first refusal. However, once they start to act they are committed, and are accountable for their actions.

Business Trustees

If you run a business, you may need to put provisions in your Will to ensure the company's continuity from the date of your death, and the succession of your share and interests in it. It may be advisable to appoint specific *business executors* to manage your business affairs. These may be your fellow partners or directors, or existing business colleagues. Or you may prefer to appoint someone external to ensure your interests are preserved and your wishes fulfilled; someone who has a good understanding of your industry or of business in general.

A number of additional factors should be considered in the appointment of executors and trustees:

Age – will they be able to cope with the amount of work involved? Unless in exceptional circumstances, you should avoid appointing people substantially older than yourself.

Location – will they be able to deal with the logistics of, for example, selling and/or clearing your house?

Financial considerations – do they have the skills to look after and invest a potentially large sum of money? They will be able to take expert advice, but will still need to capable of making decisions based on that advice.

Moral considerations – do the trustees have the same outlook on life as you? Are you satisfied they will spend money on your beneficiaries in the same way that you would have done?

Potential conflicts of interest – the offices of executor and trustee require total honesty and diligence. Their powers must be exercised in good faith in the interests of your estate and beneficiaries. The appointees must not make a profit out of acting on your behalf, and must not place themselves in a position where their duty may conflict with their personal interest.

An executor *can* also be a beneficiary of the Will. However, where there is family conflict in existence or likely to occur - or where a Trust is included in the Will - it is a good idea to appoint an independent or professional executor and trustee. One who will not be intimidated by your beneficiaries or have a conflict of interest.

STEP 2: WHO TO APPOINT AS GUARDIAN FOR YOUR CHILDREN

STEP 2: WHO TO APPOINT AS GUARDIAN FOR YOUR CHILDREN

THE SITUATION IF YOU DO NOT APPOINT A GUARDIAN

Accidents can happen to anyone, at any time, and it's a sad fact that every seven minutes a child in the UK loses a parent.

Guardianship is the legal status under which a person has *parental responsibility* for a minor child (under eighteen) following the death of one or both of the child's parents.

> *Unless you appoint guardians by making a Will, your children will become 'Wards of the State'.*

Unfortunately, it's a myth believed by many parents, that appointed god-parents, or your parents or siblings would automatically become guardians for your children on your death; in fact religion has no standing in the law, and the reality regarding family members is also very different.

Unless you appoint guardians by making a Will, your children will become *Wards of the State*. This means that Social Services will decide where they live in the immediate future, and then the courts will appoint their permanent guardians.

It's a parent's duty to make their wishes absolutely clear on this matter, by making a Will; otherwise your wishes:

a) Won't be known, and

b) Won't be carried out.

This can result in conflict that can tear families apart; with both sides fighting it out in court. One side may *win* and the other side *lose*, but in reality nobody wins - least of all your children. And you may actually have preferred your friends to care for them.

THE RIGHT TO APPOINT A GUARDIAN

A parent may appoint a guardian *only* if the parent has parental responsibility (PR) for the child. This is defined as *"all the rights, duties, power, responsibility and authority which by law a parent has in relation to the child and his property"*. However, not all parents have PR, and this can cause massive problems if the necessary guardians haven't been appointed.

The situation is that:

1. Both natural or adoptive parents have parental responsibility if they were married to each other when the child was born. If they were unmarried at that time,

then only the (birth/adoptive) mother has PR. The father, or a same-sex partner, may later acquire PR in such cases by any of the following:

- Marrying the child's mother

- Registration on the child's birth certificate

- Entering into a PR Agreement with the child's mother

- Obtaining a PR Order or a Residence Order (determining where a child will live) from the court

- Being appointed as a guardian

So for example, without appointing her child's father as guardian in her Will, a mother could inadvertently exclude her unmarried partner from automatically becoming their own child's guardian after her death.

2. A guardian has the power to appoint another guardian to replace themselves.

3. A Step-parent however; because they are not the child's parent, could not appoint a guardian for the child, unless they were acting as the appointed guardian at the time.

A guardian nominated in a Will becomes the child's guardian on the parent's death, providing either; there is no surviving parent with parental responsibility, or the deceased parent had a court appointed Residence Order for the child.

If neither of these qualifications is met, the Will appointment cannot take immediate effect. It could however take effect on the death of the surviving parent, but if both parents had appointed different guardians in their respective Wills, both appointees would have to act jointly.

This again highlights the need for taking professional advice when drafting a Will. Not only to consider the child's needs after the death of the first parent, but also after the death of the surviving parent or step-parent, and the relevant wording needs to be used in the Will to ensure the relevant provisions apply.

PROVIDING FOR GUARDIANS

The guardian's legal duty is to see that the child is *"adequately fed, clothed, housed, educated and given medical aid"*.

Leaving guidance

Guardians can be appointed in sole or joint capacity. Generally the children will go to live with the guardians, so if you want to appoint both sets of Grandparents jointly; you need to leave guidance as to how you wish this to work - such as where the children are to live. This decision should be included within the Will, and preferably more detailed guidance as to the child's upbringing left in a letter sitting with the Will. This guidance might include reference to the following; their schooling, wanting them to maintain contact with both sides of the family, the gift you would wish them to receive on their eighteenth birthday, provision of their first car, etc.

Potential conflicts of interest

The wealth of the guardian is not usually a major issue, as the deceased's estate (held in trust) will take care of the child's financial needs. How this financial support is best achieved should be carefully considered. In particular, whether or not it is advisable for the guardian to also be one of the trustees appointed in the Will (to have responsibility for looking after the child's inheritance in Trust) or whether there would be a significant conflict of interest.

Common areas of conflict include the use of Trust income for the benefit of the child, which would also assist with the guardian's own additional costs; payment of holidays, equipment which will benefit the whole household, the need for a bigger car or even a house extension. Issues which arise over the effect released Trust income has on raising the standard of living generally for the rest of the family.

If a bigger car or house extension was required, serious decisions need to be taken; such as how much Trust income compared to the guardian's funds should be used. What portion of the Trust's overall value would be utilised? What will be the ownership of the car or extension? And, will an additional loan or mortgage be required? Serious consideration must be given as to whether your guardian would realistically be able to make an unbiased decision, or whether you should appoint completely separate trustees.

SUITABILITY FOR THE ROLE

Social factors

The key factor in a parent's mind will be the selection of the most suitable person/s to undertake the role. Social factors involved usually include:

- Proximity of family relationship and location

- Age, and experience of caring for children

- Existing knowledge of, and relationship with, the child

- Suitability of their residence and their occupation

- Avoidance of disruption to education

- Religious/cultural background

As with the appointment of executors and trustees, it is important to carefully consider who to appoint. You need to discuss the matter with them - as they may not want to accept the responsibility - and also with your child, if they are of a suitable age and understanding. The court may give teenagers a choice of where they want to live if they are not happy to live with the appointed guardians, or if none have been appointed.

Primary, replacement and temporary appointments

Depending on the ages of your children, you may need to consider appointing both *primary* and *secondary or replacement* guardians. This is in case your primary guardians are unable or unwilling to act at the time they are called on, due to a change in their own circumstances.

If your primary guardian takes up the role, it is their responsibility to appoint their own replacement; as the role will not automatically pass to your own choice of replacement. This is also an important point to discuss with them; to ensure they are happy to appoint your second choice as their replacement.

There are further factors to consider if your primary guardians live overseas. Most importantly, will your child be legally allowed to enter their country to live with them? It is not always possible and so this must be checked out before making the appointment. In addition you need to consider who will look after them in the interim. It's likely to take overseas guardians some time to travel to the UK to collect your child (they may need to arrange Visas, etc.), so a *temporary* UK guardian should be appointed in these circumstances.

Provision for multiple children

> *I've yet to meet a parent who would rather have Social Services make the guardianship decision for them!*

If you have multiple children, and it would not be feasible for them to go to live with your chosen guardian, you can make provision for the guardian to move into your family home. In this case, further thought needs to be given as to when they should vacate the home. When your youngest child reached eighteen? When your oldest child is sufficiently mature to take over the role themselves?

Appointing Guardians is undoubtedly one of the most difficult decisions parents will ever have to make, particularly if both parents want their children to live with their own family members. However, I've yet to meet a parent who would rather have Social Services make the guardianship decision for them!

STEP 3: HOW TO ENSURE WHO INHERITS YOUR ESTATE

STEP 3: HOW TO ENSURE WHO INHERITS YOUR ESTATE

LIMITATIONS ON YOUR FREEDOM OF CHOICE

The impact of legislation

Since the 1830's, unlike the laws across the rest of Europe, English law provided that a person writing a Will (the testator) had *testamentary freedom*; meaning he was free to choose to whom and how his estate passed. There was however a downside, as detailed by a Judge at the time, that an English testator *"may disinherit, either wholly or partially, his children, and leave his property to strangers to gratify his spite, or to charities to gratify his pride, and we must give effect to his will, however much we may condemn the course he has pursued"*.

In the early twentieth century, prompted by disinherited spouses and children throwing themselves on the State for support, the principle of testamentary freedom was balanced by legislation. Parliament started passing Acts to allow spouses and dependants who felt they had not been properly provided for in a Will, to apply for financial provision from a deceased's estate.

Needless to say, given the pace of social change over the last century, the classes of people legally entitled to apply for *reasonable financial provision* has expanded, and now includes:

- Spouses/civil partners of the deceased

- **Former** spouses/civil partners of the deceased who have not re-married

- Any child of the deceased

- Any person who was treated as a child of the family, e.g. a step-child

- A person who was maintained by the deceased

- A cohabitant who was living with the deceased, effectively as their spouse/civil partner for two years or more

This means, if your Will does not take into account these potential applicants, a court may decide what provision to make them - rather than your estate passing under your Will as you had intended. To avoid this you really need to take professional estate planning advice.

THE EFFECT OF MARITAL STATUS

Everybody's situation, requirements and intentions are different, and can change substantially and regularly throughout their lives. For instance, in today's society, marriage is no longer seen as the lifetime commitment it once was, or even as a necessity.

Marriage or remarriage invalidates an existing Will – unless it was made *in contemplation of* the event. While divorce does not necessarily invalidate a Will it may invalidate parts of it, which will then pass via the rules of intestacy. Your ex-spouse will be deemed to have *predeceased* you in terms of any appointment they were due to take up, or any gift they were due to receive – though they can make a claim against your estate. And from the time you separate to the time you receive your *decree absolute*, they are still legally your spouse and entitled to inherit under your Will or intestacy.

> *It's an unfortunate myth that people still believe "my spouse will inherit everything."*

It's an unfortunate myth that people still believe "my spouse will inherit everything." If you don't have a valid Will this may well not be the case - depending on the value of your assets, *how* you own them, and how both your family and estate are structured.

For example, imagine you are married. You live in the South East; have three children over eighteen and your *estate* (your solely owned assets) is worth £600,000. This doesn't mean you are *rich*; after all, the bulk of your *wealth* may be tied up in your property.

Unfortunately the rules of intestacy dictate that your spouse will only receive the first £250,000 absolutely. Your adult children will immediately be entitled to fifty percent of the rest (£175,000), with the balance (£175,000) sitting *in Trust*, ultimately for your children, with your spouse receiving the interest on it during his or her lifetime.

Let us assume that the family home is in your sole name, or owned as *tenants in common* (e.g. 50:50) with your spouse and your share in it is valued at £500,000 of your £600,000 estate. Your surviving spouse may quite possibly have to sell the home to provide for your children's inheritance on your death (particularly if you have no Life Assurance) - all because you didn't think you needed to write a Will.

> *There is no such legal entity as a 'common-law spouse'.*

The situation is even worse if you are in an unmarried partnership. Contrary to popular belief, there is no such legal entity as a *common-law spouse*. With no spouse, your £600,000 estate will immediately be liable to inheritance tax. After this tax has been paid (£110,000 in this case), the balance will pass outright to your three adult children, or to your surviving parents or siblings if you have no children. And, as your partner is not entitled to any assets in your sole name, they will lose their home and will have to take your estate to court to fight for a claim for *maintenance*. This is a battle guaranteed to be both lengthy and costly with no guarantee of success. Having just lost you, this is probably not what you would have intended for them.

You could also inadvertently leave your estate to your ex-spouse!

Fred and Wilma are divorced, and each made new Wills leaving everything to their daughter Pebbles on their death. Pebbles is nineteen, single with no children and, not surprisingly, does not have a Will.

Fred and Pebbles are both involved in a car accident. Fred dies instantly, and Pebbles dies of her injuries six weeks later. Pebbles inherits Fred's estate initially, under the terms of his Will, then Wilma ultimately inherits his estate, under the rules of intestacy that apply to Pebbles' estate. And it could so easily have been avoided; if only Fred had taken professional advice, he could have made provision for just such a possibility.

PROBLEMATIC BENEFICIARIES

A common family situation is to want your estate to pass straight to your surviving spouse or partner on your death (1st death), and then to your children on the death of the survivor (2nd death). Often, however, the situation needs a lot more thought in order to enable the protection of your assets from unforeseen events.

Take, for example, the issue of 'wayward children'.

Mr and Mrs Smith have three children. Unfortunately, their youngest is a drug and alcohol dependent teenager, their middle child is a nightmare with money and his marriage and business are likely to collapse as a result. Their oldest child is single with no children, and has been very successful.

This puts Mr and Mrs Smith in an extremely difficult position. If their combined estate is given directly to their children on 2nd death, their youngest child will inherit outright by the age of twenty-five, and is likely to drink away her inheritance (or worse). Their second child is likely to lose half his inheritance to his wife on their divorce, and the rest to his creditors through bankruptcy proceedings. And their third child, having been so successful, has a substantial inheritance tax liability on his own estate, and no heirs. So how on earth do they protect their assets for - and from - their children?

Fortunately, the solution is simple: they can put a 'Trust' in their Wills. For many people just the idea of a 'Trust' sounds far too complicated – it really isn't. Leaving something 'in trust' just means leaving it with conditions, letting you keep some control even after your death. So, in the Smith's case; the children are provided for out of the Trust, without receiving the assets outright; hence the assets can't be frittered away, or claimed by an unwelcome event or third party - such as divorce, bankruptcy, or the tax man.

The situation is similar for disabled beneficiaries. They shouldn't inherit outright if they couldn't manage their own finances. And even if they are able to, any inheritance they receive over the Government permitted asset levels will result in a loss of means-tested state benefits. This doesn't just relate to the financial benefits; it includes all the support structures as well. So it's very important, for a disabled beneficiary, that their inheritance passes into a Trust and they receive provision from the Trust rather than receiving the funds outright.

CONTROLLING ASSETS FROM BEYOND THE GRAVE

Are you happy to leave your estate to your husband's next wife? Do you want your children's inheritance to be swallowed up by your wife's care fees?

A similar situation arises when couples want to ensure that if their spouse or partner should remarry or go into care after their death, their own children will ultimately inherit, and not any 'new family' or the local authority.

Are you happy to leave your estate to your husband's next wife? Do you want your children's inheritance to be swallowed up by your wife's care fees? Are you sure your surviving partner will provide for your previous children in his Will? If the answer is "NO", then you need to consider some estate planning provision.

Once again, the use of a Trust is an effective solution.

Mr and Mrs Jones have remarried in later life. They have no children together, though each have adult children from their previous marriages whom they ultimately want to receive their own estate; in the meantime they want to ensure their surviving spouse benefits from all their assets.

They can each leave their own estate into Trust in their Wills, ultimately for the benefit of their own children, but with their surviving spouse being given a 'life tenancy'. This means that on Mr Jones' death, his estate will be held 'in trust' for his children, with Mrs Jones receiving all the income from the Trust during her lifetime. She can continue to live in his property, or can move or downsize. She can even receive lump sums of capital from the Trust, or she could borrow the capital instead, which will then be repaid back to his Trust on her death.

Even if Mrs Jones remarries or goes into Residential Care, Mr Jones' Trust remains secure for his children. It would pass to them upon Mrs Jones' death, rather than to her new husband or to pay for her care home fees.

So, by utilising effective estate planning provisions, you can control who receives your assets, what they receive, when and how - even from beyond the grave!

STEP 4: HOW TO AVOID PAYING UNNECESSARILY INHERITANCE TAX

STEP 4: HOW TO AVOID PAYING UNNECESSARILY INHERITANCE TAX

THE WEALTH AND STEALTH TAX

Inheritance Tax (IHT) is triggered when, in its simplest terms, an asset is transferred from one party to another - usually on death. Effectively, it's your *legacy* to the Government (HMRC), due because of an excess of value in your estate. What people don't realise, however, is that it is potentially a 'voluntary' tax if you plan for it.

Traditionally most people in the UK haven't given great consideration to inheritance tax, believing it only affected the rich. This is no longer the case, and many issues being faced by families today are a direct result of being dragged into the IHT net by stealth means. Primarily because their principal asset - their home - has increased in value at a greater rate than the financial threshold at which IHT kicks in.

WHAT IT MEANS FOR YOU

On their death every individual has a *tax-free allowance* or threshold, above which their assets may incur inheritance tax at a rate of forty percent (40%), depending on who they leave them to. This allowance - known as a *Nil Rate Band* (NRB) - is the value on which a nil-rate of tax is due and has been fixed by the Government at the current rate of £325,000 until 2019.

You can make a gift to anyone in your Will, up to the value of your nil-rate band, without inheritance tax being due. You can also make gifts to certain people and organisations without having to pay IHT.

These tax-exempt beneficiaries are:

- Your spouse/civil partner, as long as they are considered to be a UK national (more on this later, in Step 5)

- A UK or EU registered charity

- Some national institutions; such as museums, universities and the National Trust

- A mainstream UK political party

The effect of inheritance tax is that, potentially, forty percent of the value of your assets in excess of the nil-rate band will have to be paid to HMRC within six months of your death. There are many factors affecting if, when, and how much IHT is payable; including:

Gifts between spouses

If you are married and you leave everything to your spouse on your death (1st death), or into Trust for their benefit, there will be no IHT to be paid until their death (2nd death). This relief came about after significant changes to legislation in October 2007, so anybody with a Will drafted before that date should review it as soon as possible.

Since October 2007 the situation for spouses has definitely changed for the better. Not only are transfers of assets between yourself and your spouse tax-free - if you leave your estate to your spouse (or in Trust for them) - they will also *inherit* your nil-rate band (£325,000) to add to their own. This means on 2nd death, there will be up to two NRB's (£650,000* tax-free from your combined estates) to leave to your children or other taxable beneficiaries; saving £130,000 in Tax!

Even so, it has been worked out that a gift of £1m that passes through four generations will generate inheritance tax receipts of £880,000 for HMRC - due to it being taxed on each death!

Gifts between unmarried partners are not tax-exempt; meaning anything over the nil-rate band will attract a forty percent charge to IHT on 1st death. Also if you leave your estate to your partner outright, you will have used up your NRB and it will not be accrued. As a result, they will only have their own £325,000 NRB to leave tax-free on 2nd death.

However, in these circumstances you can protect your NRB, e.g. for your children. You can leave it in Trust for the benefit of your partner during their life. Then on your partner's death, both your NRB (in Trust) and their own NRB will pass to your children tax-free.

The *7 Year Rule* affecting lifetime gifts

One of the complications to the IHT issue is that gifts you make during your lifetime can have an effect on the amount of available NRB on your death. Although every individual can leave £325,000 tax-free to anyone on their death, HMRC looked at ways it could increase its tax receipts, and as a result brought in the *7 Year Rule*.

This rule dictates that the value of any gifts you made in the seven years prior to your death will reduce the amount of your NRB available to leave on your death by the same amount. For example:

> Widower Roger gave each of his three children £75,000 for Christmas in 2010. He died unexpectedly two years later and, as a result, his £325,000 NRB was reduced by the three £75,000 legacies; leaving only £100,000 tax-free to pass on after his death.

Essentially this means any gifts you make to individuals in your lifetime, will only truly be exempt from IHT if you live for seven years after making the gift.

The above scenario is more of an inconvenience than a major issue, as there is still a tax-free benefit available on death. It becomes a major issue where the lifetime gifts accrue to more than the NRB, such as in the following example.

> If Roger had instead given each of his children £175,000 in 2010, the total gift of £525,000 would be over his NRB. So the additional £200,000 would be liable to IHT on his death in 2012 and the tax liability would fall on the beneficiaries of the gift!

This is where lifetime planning can have a major impact on how your Will works, and why professional advice should be sought.

Gifts made into Trust during your lifetime, e.g. to finance your grandchildren's education, can be equally problematical. In addition to the 7 Year Rule, you can only put a maximum of the NRB into Trust every seven years while you are alive. Anything over the NRB is liable to an immediate twenty percent (20%) lifetime IHT payment. For example:

Roger set up a Trust for his three children instead of gifting the money to them outright, so he could retain control of the use of the funds during his lifetime. He transferred the £525,000 into the Trust, and found himself faced with a tax bill of twenty percent on the £200,000 in excess of the NRB – requiring an immediate payment of £40,000.

AVOIDING INHERITANCE TAX

> "Inheritance Tax is paid by people who distrust their heirs more than they dislike the Inland Revenue."

In the words of former Chancellor, Lord Selwyn Gummer, "Inheritance Tax is paid by people who distrust their heirs more than they dislike the Inland Revenue."

> *Avoid leaving the Government a legacy in your Will.*

Like most people, you would probably like to avoid leaving the Government a legacy in your Will. Particularly if your assets were accumulated after you have already paid a substantial amount of tax, e.g. on earnings, National Insurance, VAT, Stamp Duty.

So, to reduce IHT, unmarried couples should use a Trust in their Wills to preserve their NRB, and married couples should leave everything to each other or in Trust for the benefit of the survivor.

There is an additional strategy to reduce IHT through your Will; by leaving a minimum of ten percent (10%) of your net estate to charity. Leaving a ten percent (10%) gift to charity reduces the forty percent (40%) IHT due on your taxable estate, by ten percent (10%), to thirty-six percent (36%). This often results in your other beneficiaries receiving more of your estate than if there was no charity gift – so give to charity rather than the Government!

There are also some *quick wins* available during your lifetime to reduce IHT on your death (without spending everything!). Particularly in light of the 7 Year Rule.

Lifetime tax planning – *exempt gifts*

Some gifts made during your lifetime are totally exempt from IHT calculations, provided accurate records are kept to prove the exemption.

- Annual gift

  You can give away gifts worth up to £3,000 in total in each

tax year. Any unused part of the £3,000 exemption in one year (only) can be carried over to the next year.

- Small gifts

  You can make gifts up to the value of £250 to as many individuals as you like in any one tax year. However, if the amount is greater than £250 the exemption on the gift is lost altogether. You cannot use your small gifts allowance together with any other exemption when giving to the same person.

- Wedding/civil partnership gifts

  These are exempt from IHT, subject to certain limits:

  a. Parents can each give cash or gifts worth £5,000

  b. Grandparents and great grandparents can each give cash or gifts worth £2,500

  c. Anyone else can give cash or gifts worth £1,000

- Regular gifts or payments that are part of your *normal expenditure*

  Any regular gifts you make out of your after-tax income, (not gifts of your capital) are exempt from IHT. These gifts will only qualify if, after making them, you have enough income left to maintain your normal lifestyle.

  These include:

  a. Monthly or other regular payments to someone

  b. Regular gifts for Christmas, birthdays, or anniversaries

    c. Regular premiums on a life insurance policy – yours or someone else's

You can also make exempt maintenance payments to:

    a. Your spouse/civil partner

    b. Your ex-spouse/former civil partner

    c. Relatives dependent on you because of old age or infirmity

    d. Your children - including adopted children and step-children - under eighteen or in full-time education

Lifetime tax planning – *Life Assurance*

The best way of minimizing the effect of an unavoidable inheritance tax liability is to ensure you have sufficient Life Assurance to cover the tax. Otherwise, your unfortunate family could find themselves having to sell the family home to pay the tax bill on your death.

However; if you do have Life Assurance or a company death-in-service policy, it is vitally important to ensure it doesn't pay out into your estate and become liable to IHT itself. Nor should it fall into your surviving spouse/partner's estate, for the same reason.

Life policies, along with Pensions, should be set up to pay out into a Trust - which you set up during your lifetime to receive the payments after your death. Using a Trust in this way not only ensures the payment is not subject to forty percent IHT. It also ensures the funds do not get frozen during the probate process and are thus immediately available to your family.

There are many legal ways of avoiding - rather than evading - inheritance tax. Or for putting in place provisions to meet the tax bill so your family aren't forced to sell assets. Whatever your individual circumstances, solutions are available and specialist advice should be sought.

IHT is a tax liability which can be planned for - don't leave it too long though.

* Depending on whether they have made any taxable lifetime gifts in the seven years prior to their death.

STEP 5: HOW TO DEAL WITH FOREIGN ISSUES

STEP 5: HOW TO DEAL WITH FOREIGN ISSUES

THE FOUR FOREIGN ISSUES AND THEIR IMPACT

When succession planning, there are four common problems you may face with regards to foreign issues; three relate to your assets and the fourth relates to your spouse.

The issues are:

1. Probate delays

2. The possibility of assets being taxed twice

3. Limitations to your freedom of succession choice

4. Limits on tax-free assets left to a foreign spouse

Probate delays

If you've ever read an English Will you will know it is drafted in *legalese*. There are two reasons for this.

Firstly, most people are not fluent in legal jargon. So when your executors read your Will and can't understand a word of it, they take it to the nearest solicitor to deal with it for them - solicitors make a lot of money out of probate!

The second reason is that the *terms and conditions* within your Will, known as *precedents*, have been laid down over centuries. So, if there is any contest over your Will, the legal experts who sort it out in court rely on these tried and tested precedents to reach their conclusions as to what you had intended.

If your UK Will also covers your foreign assets; picture the situation in the foreign lawyer's office when your Will lands on their desk. They'll take one look at it and - baffled by the English legal waffle - will consign it to the bottom of their in-tray. And every time it comes to the top, it'll go straight back to the bottom!

Your estate cannot be distributed until the deed of probate has been granted, which requires all your assets to have been dealt with. The delays caused by the foreign lawyer will hold up the whole of your estate. I know people who have been waiting over three years for a loved one's probate to be sorted out; precisely for this reason. And, all that time, they've been unable to access the deceased's bank accounts or other assets. How would your family fare in such a situation?

The possibility of assets being taxed twice

Liability to UK inheritance tax depends on your *domicile* at the time you make a *transfer of assets*; this could be a gift during your lifetime or assets passing under your Will.

Domicile is a legal concept. It is not possible to list all the factors that affect your domicile, and for succession purposes you are not necessarily domiciled in the country where you live. Domicile is different from nationality or residence.

Everybody is born with a *domicile of origin*, which is normally acquired from your father when you are born. It may not be the country in which you are born. For example, if you were born in France while your father was working there, but his permanent home is in the UK, your domicile of origin is the UK.

You can legally acquire a new domicile, a *domicile of choice*. To do so, you must:

- Leave the country in which you are now domiciled and settle in another country, and

- Provide strong evidence that you intend to live there permanently or indefinitely

Living in another country for a long time, although an important factor, does not prove you have acquired a new domicile.

For inheritance tax purposes, there is a concept of *deemed* UK domicile. This means even if you are not domiciled in the UK under the considerations above, you will be treated as UK domiciled for inheritance tax purposes at the time of a transfer of assets if either:

a. You had been domiciled in the UK within the three years immediately before the transfer (i.e. death within three years of making a change to a *domicile of choice*), or

b. You lived in the UK for at least seventeen of the twenty years immediately before the transfer

As a rule of thumb:

- If you are a UK domicile, then UK inheritance tax applies to your worldwide assets. But the succession laws on foreign *immovable property* - generally land and building - fall under the foreign jurisdiction (i.e. the law of the country where your foreign property is situated)

- If you are a foreign domicile living in the UK, then UK inheritance tax generally applies only to your UK assets

However, foreign jurisdictions often take a very different approach to the concept of domicile for tax purposes, and apply their own tests. For example:

- In Belgium, China, and Chile, the tax situation is decided on whether you are predominantly resident in that country

- In Germany, Greece, Italy, and Spain, it is based on nationality

What this means is that if you have a connection to more than one jurisdiction, they might all claim the right to tax your estate.

The Government has entered into *Double-Taxation Treaties* with many foreign jurisdictions. This helps prevent assets being taxed by two countries if both deem themselves to have the right to tax the same property when a death occurs or a gift is made.

Limitations to your freedom of succession choice

In twenty-six out of twenty-seven EU countries, a portion of a deceased's estate is reserved for their surviving spouse and children. This can cause significant problems on your death if you leave provisions in your Will that conflict with the succession laws of the country where the property is situated. And, as we know, problems mean delays in gaining probate.

Limits on tax-free assets left to a foreign spouse

As established earlier, you can gift or leave all your assets to your spouse tax-free. PROVIDED your spouse is UK domiciled. Where the recipient spouse is foreign domiciled, the tax-free transfer is restricted to £55,000 plus the nil-rate-band. For example:

Fred, a lonely and affluent pensioner, married a Thai girl he met on holiday in 1998. They lived happily together in the UK until his death in January 2013 and he left everything to his wife in his Will. As she had been married to Fred for only fourteen years, she was not deemed to be domiciled in the UK for IHT purposes.

Fred's estate amounted to £500,000 after the deduction of debts due on his death. The tax free gift to his wife amounted to £55,000 plus his NRB of £325,000 - a total of £380,000. The balance, £120,000, was taxed at forty percent, giving the taxman a gift of £24,000.

The reason for this restriction is because; the Government wants to remove the possibility of your foreign-domiciled surviving spouse selling up after your death, and leaving the country with the sale proceeds. As if they did, HMRC would have lost any IHT that may become due on their future death.

HOW BEST TO DEAL WITH THE FOREIGN ISSUES

The first three issues – probate delays, double taxation, and freedom of succession choice - can be dealt with quite simply; with some simple upfront planning. An English Will is bound by the laws of England and Wales and, as such, if you own any property outside England and Wales you should ideally have a Will wherever that property is situated.

This is essential when dealing with overseas jurisdictions. If your UK Will only deals with your UK estate, the Grant of Probate will not be delayed by a foreign lawyer; however long they take to deal with your overseas assets.

When briefing a foreign lawyer to draft your foreign Will it is essential to discuss the relevant tax situation in the country, and any local succession restrictions. In many cases a UK domicile may be able to *over-ride* the local succession rules, provided the Will is drafted to reflect that.

Equally importantly, your new foreign Will must not have the standard clause "revoking all other Wills made by me" as this would revoke your existing UK Will. In the same way, your UK Will must not revoke a foreign Will. The following table provides the key points to raise when instructing a foreign lawyer while drafting your foreign Will.

Checklist for instructing a foreign Lawyer to draft your foreign Will.

1	Tell them you have an existing Will or Wills dealing with all your assets except those in the local jurisdiction. Ideally, give them a copy of your UK Will.
2	Tell them that you want the Will limited to your foreign property, and that it must not revoke your Wills covering any other jurisdiction.
3	Ask about the succession laws within their jurisdiction, and if there are any *fixed inheritance* laws. If so, ask if there any ways of circumventing those provisions.
4	Ask who will deal with the transfer of your property after death, i.e. will it be done by executors or the beneficiaries? If the work is done by executors, who could/should be appointed? Is it feasible to appoint the same executors as in your UK Will?
5	Ask them to explain the tax position on death. Bearing in mind your foreign property will be treated as part of your UK estate for Inheritance Tax purposes. Are there tax agreements applicable between them and the UK to avoid tax being paid twice?
6	Ask whether there are any additional costs; such as providing for an English translation or registrations in the local jurisdiction.

Tax-free increases for a foreign domiciled spouse

In 2012 the Government indicated its intentions to increase the value of tax-free gifts your foreign spouse can receive from April 2013. Increasing the current tax-free limit of £55,000 to the level of the incumbent nil-rate band; meaning your foreign spouse could receive double the NRB on your death.

There may be lifetime planning provisions that can assist with the *foreign spouse* situation, e.g. how you buy and own assets, the types of investments held, and other considerations which can vastly reduce the amount of IHT that would be payable on 1st death. So if this is your situation you need to take specialist advice - sooner rather than later.

STEP 6: HOW TO CATER FOR A LOSS OF MENTAL CAPACITY

STEP 6: HOW TO CATER FOR A LOSS OF MENTAL CAPACITY

THE IMPLICATIONS OF LOSING MENTAL CAPACITY

It's not unreasonable to believe that if a loved one were to lose mental capacity (the ability to make their own decisions) – perhaps through an illness, accident, dementia, or a stroke - their family would have full powers to look after all their interests. The reality is very different.

Unless you put the right provisions in place while you are able to make your own decisions, if you lose this ability, your entire life will be controlled by the State. A secret court will freeze all your assets (including your joint and business assets) and the court, rather than your family, will decide where you will live, what levels of treatment you will receive, and even what your money can be spent on.

It sounds far-fetched doesn't it? But in 2007 the Government set up the little-known Court of Protection to act in the interests of people considered too mentally incapacitated to act on their own behalf.

The Court of Protection hears over 23,000 cases a year, always sitting in private, and with no right for families to appeal against its decisions. There are over 60,000 mentally impaired *clients* registered with the court, and they had no choice in the matter. Using far-reaching powers, the court has taken control of more than £4 billion of their assets - against the wishes of their relatives - even forcing furious families to pay to access their own joint bank accounts.

Your family must apply to the court, to be appointed to act on your behalf as the court's *deputy*, via the civil servants at the Office of the Public Guardian (OPG). It is by no means guaranteed they will be appointed. The court will investigate the full background of your loved ones to decide whether or not they consider them *fit to run your affairs*. If not, the court is free to make its own appointment.

Once appointed, the deputy is answerable to the OPG and they charge an annual fee to supervise the deputy's activities. The court maintains control of the client's finances, which means the deputy (whether a relative or not) must get authorisation for any decisions they make on your behalf - even to pay expenses such as rent and household bills. And for every decision the court makes, it charges an additional fee.

The typical costs incurred by a client as a result of coming under the control of the Court of Protection include:

- A commencement fee (£240)

- Deputy appointment fees (£315)

- Annual supervision fees (up to £800)

- Administration fees (£190-£240) – for any decision the court makes

- An account fee (£100) – as all funds are transferred into the court's account

- Transaction fees (£60-£540) – any time a payment is made, including your normal direct debits

- Accountants fees - to produce annual report and accounts, and finally

- A winding-up fee (£290)

And these fees will continue to be charged until you either recover, or die.

> *The Court of Protection's primary role is to protect **you** from your family - in order to protect **itself** from you recovering and suing it for letting your family spend your money!*

You could be forgiven for thinking; the Court of Protection's primary role is to protect **you** from your family - in order to protect **itself** from you recovering and suing it for letting your family spend your money!

The families - whose lives have effectively also been taken over by the Court of Protection - see it as a cruel, intrusive, expensive, bureaucratic and legal nightmare. And in its treatment of deputies the court does not distinguish between a close family member and a virtual stranger. Yet all this can be avoided very easily.

THE SOLUTION

Lasting Powers of Attorney (LPAs)

Lasting Powers of Attorney are documents you make while you have sufficient mental capacity, to appoint people (the *Attorneys*) to manage your (personal and business) *property and financial affairs,* and your *health and welfare,* should you become unable to manage them yourself.

Traditionally people think of LPAs as being for old people suffering from dementia, but they should be a very serious consideration for every adult. I draft most LPAs for younger people who own property, or run their own business, or have children. They recognise the need to provide for their families and their businesses in the event of a life-changing event, which could happen to anybody at any time. For example, you might have a road accident, slip over and hit your head, suffer a stroke, etc.

The list goes on. But the practical upshot is that any of these things can affect your mental capacity to such an extent that you can no longer make decisions for yourself. A recent survey by Age UK revealed one in four people in the UK are currently suffering from a significant loss of mental capacity - and far from all of them are elderly. So you need to appoint people you would trust to make decisions in your best interests, before such a situation befalls you, to avoid falling prey to the Court of Protection.

Without LPAs you could find yourself in a situation similar to Mr & Mrs Jones:

Mr and Mrs Jones have joint bank accounts, they own their house jointly, and Mr Jones' salary is paid into their joint account. Out of the blue, Mr Jones' has a stroke, loses mental capacity and is left paralysed down one side of his body. As a result Mrs Jones may need work done on their home, or to move home, to accommodate Mr Jones' condition. But she can no longer make that decision because they own their property jointly and their joint assets are frozen. Their joint bank accounts are also frozen, so Mrs Jones can't even access her own money in the account.

The Court of Protection will decide who will be their deputy, to make decisions for Mr Jones, and it won't necessarily be Mrs Jones. It could be a solicitor or the local authority - a total stranger who has never known or even met Mr Jones - but who will effectively be running both of their lives, even though Mrs Jones has full mental capacity.

It is such a mind-numbing scenario. Because when you're dead, you're dead - the probate might take six to twelve months and then it's over. But following his stroke, Mr Jones could live for another thirty, forty, or fifty years. Even if Mrs Jones is appointed as the court's deputy, she will still have to go to a government body to ask permission to spend the money in their joint account - until Mr Jones either recovers, or dies.

These rules were originally brought in because the predecessor to the LPA - the Enduring Power of Attorney (EPA) - was horribly abused. Typically, Mrs Smith might have moved into a care home where an unscrupulous carer could have said, "Just sign here Mrs Smith." Then gone to the bank to clear out Mrs Smith's account. And there was nobody there to police it.

But unfortunately, the Government's remedy did not include educating people to its implications. This has left families and businesses unable to manage their own affairs. Without LPAs in place, their only alternative is to report to anonymous civil servants by telephone. The civil servants will make decisions for them; charge them £800 a year simply for being available; and charge potentially thousands of pounds a year to make decisions that your loved ones or business partners would do as a matter of course.

Returning to the Jones'. If they had each spent a few hundred pounds and drafted LPAs before Mr Jones had a stroke, they could have appointed each other - possibly with their children as replacements - to be legally entitled to manage all their affairs. Without any government interference.

The annual costs incurred dealing with the Court of Protection and OPG are far greater than the one-off costs for drafting and registering Lasting Powers of Attorney. Unfortunately most people just don't know about them – until it's too late.

LPAs for Business

Having your family's lives controlled by the Court of Protection is a sad and ridiculous state of affairs on a personal level; but it could be terminal to your Business. Hence LPAs should be an absolute essential for anybody that runs a company.

If a company director or partner has a stroke or an accident and loses the mental capacity to make decisions (or sign pay cheques), it is vitally important the company doesn't have to ask the court to agree all management decisions.

The choice of attorney you appoint to deputise for you must be appropriate. Your spouse or child might be perfect at making domestic decisions, but be a total nightmare when it comes to running your company.

You can have separate LPAs to appoint different attorneys for different tasks. For example, your spouse and children to look after your personal affairs, and your fellow business partners /directors to look after business affairs.

And best of all, if an LPA is being put in place to protect your business, it's a bona fide business expense.

STEP 7: HOW TO ENSURE YOUR BUSINESS SURVIVES YOU

STEP 7: HOW TO ENSURE YOUR BUSINESS SURVIVES YOU

THE IMPACT OF DEATH ON YOUR BUSINESS

If you've spent years building up your business, you'll want to know for certain that it's in safe hands after you're gone.

Many of the same considerations apply in terms of your Will as they do for Lasting Powers of Attorney. Because if you're running your own business, whether you lose your mental capacity or die, your business might cease to exist if you haven't appointed the right people to take over in your absence.

Will your business survive you?

If you are a sole trader, your business will cease to exist on your death and any business assets will be frozen until after probate; unless you make specific provision in your Will for it to be continued from the time of your death.

The death or loss of mental capacity of a partner will dissolve a business partnership, even if there are three or more partners. This is a very unsatisfactory situation, which can only be avoided by drafting a legally-binding agreement between all the partners that makes provision for what should happen before such an event occurs.

The situation with a limited company (Ltd) or limited liability partnership (LLP) is different as each of them is a *legal entity* in its own right. The death or loss of capacity of a shareholder or partner may not terminate the business, as a part-ownership would pass via the Will on death, and Attorneys appointed under a Lasting Power of Attorney could take over in the event of a loss of mental capacity.

However, a death may necessitate a change in directors in the case of a limited company, which must have at least one named director in place. Or it may necessitate a change in partners in the case of an LLP, which must have two named partners in place. If not, both a limited company and an LLP would become void.

The situations above need not create havoc for your business, provided you put the right provisions in place during your lifetime. Provisions that will come into effect in the event that you lose mental capacity or die, that give the relevant powers to your attorneys or to the executors and trustees in your Will.

The importance of having the right business documentation

Depending on any restrictions or conditions laid down in your company documents - Articles of Association (Articles), Partnership Agreements, or Shareholder's Agreements - the provisions you might have made or intended to instigate through your Will, may not actually be possible.

> *Do you even have a Shareholder's or Partnership Agreement?*

Do you even have a Shareholder's or Partnership Agreement? The remarkable thing is how few people have even considered how vital such a document is - often until it's too late. Not to have the essential agreement between your business owners or partners, set out in a legally binding contract, can be fatal to your business – before or after your death.

Whether a business is carried on through a limited company or a partnership, the lack of a contract between owners or partners can have really serious consequences. Without the right documentation, if an owner or partner loses mental capacity or dies, or there is disagreement about some aspect of running the business, it usually leads to protracted and expensive litigation. And of course, the more successful the business becomes, the more important these issues will be.

A Partnership Agreement sets out the details of the partnership - its partners, their profit shares, capital contributions and, most crucially, what happens if one of them dies or has to leave the business. Without such an agreement, there is no proper record of some very major questions; such as who owns the business, who is entitled to the profits and who is liable for the losses.

It is a legally binding agreement that acts as a *rule book*, ensuring each partner knows where they stand and what is expected of them. In the absence of a partnership agreement, the Partnership Act 1890 becomes the legislation that binds the partnership, and legislation as old as this has little context in the modern world.

A Shareholders' Agreement is a contract setting out the terms on which two or more people are involved in a business as directors and/or shareholders. It supplements the company's Articles, and is essential to protect the position of anyone who is not the majority shareholder in the company.

Unless constrained by a Shareholders' Agreement, shareholders with a simple majority of votes have very wide powers under company law. Without requiring any consent from the other shareholders, they can:

- Appoint new directors (perhaps their friends or family members)

- Remove any director (including other shareholders)

- Vote themselves a pay rise (which other shareholders or directors don't get), or

- Issue more shares (diluting the other shareholders' ownership)

Among the most important areas to consider, are the rules that apply when a shareholder wants to transfer their shares and what can happen to them when the shareholder dies. These can be set out either in the Articles or in a Shareholders' Agreement.

Many companies' Articles give the directors discretion to reject any transfer by a majority decision. You may prefer alternative provisions; such as pre-emption provisions (giving the other shareholders a first option to buy the shares), free transfers to members of the shareholder's family, or for all transfers to require the consent of all shareholders. The decision as to what is applicable for your business may depend on a variety of considerations.

PROVISIONS YOU MUST MAKE

Having the right business documentation in place is imperative to ensure that your interests, as well of those of your family and business, are provided for after your death. It doesn't matter what provisions your Will makes, if your company documentation provides for something else to happen, the Will provisions will fail.

In addition, if your company documents include the wrong type of provisions, you could be landing your estate with a substantial unnecessary tax bill, for example:

Retain tax-free allowances

If your business is a trading company, it may qualify for *Business Property Relief* (BPR) on the transfer of shares in certain circumstances - a one hundred percent reduction in inheritance tax, to zero. However, if your Articles create an absolute *contract for sale* of your shares on your death, your family will lose forty percent of the proceeds of sale to the tax man - simply because you hadn't reviewed your documentation.

Avoid leaving your shares to the 'wrong' people.

For example:

Mr Thomson is MD of a company in which he is the majority fifty percent shareholder. He has three fellow-directors who are also minority shareholders. Mr Thomson's family have no understanding of, or interest in, the business whatsoever. Unfortunately, on his death, his Will gifted his business shares to Mrs Thomson and his two adult children.

How will his fellow directors cope with this situation? They certainly don't want to be working with the Thomson family - who are now legally entitled to decide how the company is run.

And, while the Thomson's are happily drawing dividends and salaries from the business, the company can't afford to appoint another director to take over the late Mr Thomson's duties. Neither can the company or its remaining directors afford to buy the family out; even if they did all want to sell - which they don't.

Yet the situation could have been so different, if only the directors had taken some advice.

Mr Thomson's situation is all too common. In fact it is typically the *default position* in the vast majority of Wills I have reviewed for business owners; simply because nobody has ever discussed with them the implications of making appropriate provisions - on all the people they leave behind.

Company *Key Man* Life Assurance

Nobody had ever talked to Mr Thomson and his fellow shareholders about the potential for the company setting up Life Assurance policies to pay out on the death of one of the named key employees; to provide the money to buy his shares from his family. Nor had anyone discussed with them combining the Life Assurance with the use of a written agreement; which would ensure that, whether the remaining directors wished to buy his shares or the Thomson family to sell them, the other party was duty-bound to agree.

Leave your shares to a Trust

Likewise, nobody had advised them on the possibility of each person leaving their shares into a Trust on their death, rather than directly to their family. By doing so, along with giving specific *business continuity* authority in their Wills, they could appoint *business trustees* (which may include their fellow directors) to make the necessary business decisions unhindered; from the time of their death until such a time as the shares were sold.

In addition, Mr Thomson had not been advised that the use of a Trust to receive his shares would reduce potential inheritance tax on their later sale. A Trust would not only ensure no inheritance tax was payable on the shares on his death, it would also protect the proceeds of sale on the future death of Mrs Thomson, or his children. This is because the death of a Trust beneficiary does not initiate an inheritance tax charge, as it would if the funds were sitting in that beneficiary's own estate.

With some professional advice to ensure careful business succession planning during your lifetime, you can protect your business in the event of your death, or loss of mental capacity. This will produce a *win-win* situation for your fellow directors, shareholders, partners, and employees; as well as for your family.

The essentials are:

- Make Lasting Powers of Attorney in case you should lose mental capacity

- Review your company documentation to ensure it will deliver what you want, and

- Put in place an up to date, valid, carefully considered, professionally drafted Will.

CONCLUSION

CONCLUSION

Your Will is not only one of the most important documents you will ever write; it is also the largest cheque you will ever write – it disposes of all your assets!

Nearly seventy percent of people in the UK die without a Will. And, of those that have Wills, some twenty-eight percent are found to have major flaws that totally change the way assets are distributed.

There are so many things you need to be aware of in order to make sure your family, your assets, and your business are secure after you're gone - just getting started can be intimidating.

Maybe you have children from past relationships; or someone else could have a legal claim on your estate? Perhaps you have an inheritance tax problem; or a business succession challenge?

Whatever your situation, I hope this book has clarified what you need to both consider and prepare; to ensure you avoid the perils, pitfalls and problems that most people unwittingly make.

You should by now have a good understanding of:

- How to ensure you appoint the right people to the relevant roles

- How you can ensure your children are taken care of

- How to ensure your assets go where, when and how you want them to

- How to avoid paying unnecessary Inheritance Tax

- How to cater for foreign complications

- Why every adult should have Lasting Powers of Attorney, and

- How to make sure your Business continues to prosper after you're gone

So, what are you waiting for?

Before you meet your Maker, make sure you meet your Will-Maker!

ABOUT THE
AUTHOR

ABOUT THE AUTHOR

Rachael Rodgers is the owner of Heir Tight Wills & Estate Planning Ltd, based in Kent and covering London and the South East, dealing predominantly with clients referred to her by various professional introducers; financial advisors, accountants and solicitors.

Rachael explains how she got into Will writing in the first place:

> *"Having spent many years in Business Development looking after the needs (and protecting the assets) of large corporate organisations, I was employed in the city when the bombs went off in July 2005. This was my 'light-bulb moment'. I didn't live in London; I didn't need to work in London - and I didn't have a Will!"*

It was in researching the solutions for her own requirements that Rachael got *hooked* on the whole concept of Estate Planning.

Rachael joined the industry's largest professional organisations; the Institute of Professional Will Writers (IPW), and Society of Will Writers (SWW), and put herself through their full range of College courses. She then found herself a very experienced mentor, who guided her through her ongoing learning process.

In a few short years Rachael was running her own company and drafting all the documents herself. Her reputation spread, and she was taken on by a firm of Solicitors with branches across Kent and London to provide Will writing services to their business and consumer clients.

Rachael went on to further her expertise; gaining the highest qualification in Will preparation and drafting (unlike many Solicitors), through the industry's leading body STEP – the Society of Trust and Estate Practitioners. This has enabled her to expand her reach, by utilising the services of specially selected professionals to provide the regulated services her clients require, but which she herself is unable to supply.

Rachael explains her role as:

"I am a qualified, fully insured, specialist in Wills and Estate Planning. To use a medical analogy, I am not a generalist GP who covers a large variety of topics, but the specialist they would refer you to when they know you need something more specific.

I visit my clients personally, in the comfort of their own home or office, at a time to suit them. I advise them on the relevant options – in plain English, not legal jargon - to provide solutions to their own unique circumstances.

I am a one-stop-shop facility for my clients; working with a range of specialist financial advisors, accountants, company lawyers and barristers, to provide assistance in areas where they do not have the relevant provision themselves. I make sure the end-result exactly meets their objectives in a legally heir-tight fashion; so they can rest assured they have exactly what they need and that their documents have been drafted to the highest standards.

Being a full member of the IPW and the SWW, and an Affiliate of STEP, ensures I keep up to date with the numerous changes in the industry as they happen. It also ensures I adhere to the highest codes of conduct, and I am required to have £2m of professional indemnity insurance cover for my clients' protection - though I have never had to call on it!

I trade on four things - professionalism, credibility, integrity and transparency."

For more Estate Planning assistance please visit my website, or contact me directly to find out how I can help.

www.heir-tight-wills.co.uk

e: info@heir-tight-wills.co.uk

t: 0845 519 7585

TESTIMONIALS

TESTIMONIALS

"Rachael Rodgers recognizes that advice needs to be matched with the ability to sensitively manage each individual's needs for a successful outcome. I was referred to Rachael by my IFA and she has supported me with a one-stop-solution for my Will, Trusts and Lasting Powers of Attorney, as well as bringing in a specialist solicitor and barrister to advise on my private company structure. Wills can feel difficult to map, and the more complex the circumstances, the greater the need for the clarity, precision, and the ever-friendly authority of someone like Rachael. And she'll be on your case - to deliver her commitments and ensure the same from you! Excellent service and great support."

Andrew Brindley Davies - CRICKET Brand Communications - www.cricket-ltd.com

The service was excellent. It was significantly better than the service provided through a local solicitor for an earlier Will and EPA. Rachael was very professional and patient in responding to any questions I raised. The LPAs were duly registered with the Court of Protection without problem."
Trevor Watkins - retired, Bexleyheath

Rachael's review of our existing Wills revealed major weakness in both, missed by our solicitors, which could have been catastrophic in the future. She gave a comprehensive and professional service, explained things in plain English, and produced a very satisfactory outcome. Highly recommended!"
Ian James - Sourceout Ltd, Chislehurst

" I have known Rachael for several years. She is very organised, knowledgeable, and professional. Her mild manner has meant she patiently waited for the right moment to provide my family with her professional Will writing and Estate Planning services. Working to meet a tight deadline - my Charity Sky Dive for Help for Heroes - she completed our Wills within 24 hours. My wife's worries were properly sorted out and the (just in case) planning was not called on.

I have, and will continue to, recommend Rachael as the best in her field. Previously we were with old-style family solicitors. Remember, if you don't do it properly, after your parachute has not opened your family will find that they have to pay through the nose."

Robert Murray Willis - Castleacre Insurance Services Ltd., Tunbridge Wells

I met Rachael at a breakfast meeting where she was a guest speaker, providing insights into problems arising when you die intestate or, worse, survive with limited mental capacity but without powers of attorney.

She visited my husband and I, at our convenience in our office, and we discussed with her what we wanted to achieve. Rachael made sure we fully understood the provisions we were putting in place, and provided the documents in a timely manner, even coming back to witness the signing. She advised us on how to store them, and how to use the LPAs if needed.

We have peace of mind that our Wills are now set out to provide for our wishes. And with LPAs, we can look after each other's interests without outside interference. I am happy to recommend Rachael."

Christine Collen - C&C Business Services, West Wickham

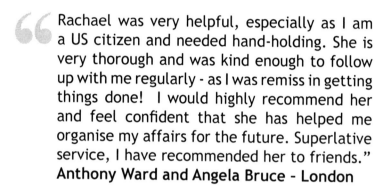

Rachael was very helpful, especially as I am a US citizen and needed hand-holding. She is very thorough and was kind enough to follow up with me regularly - as I was remiss in getting things done! I would highly recommend her and feel confident that she has helped me organise my affairs for the future. Superlative service, I have recommended her to friends."
Anthony Ward and Angela Bruce - London

All aspects relating to our Wills and LPAs were expertly provided, with sound advice relating to our son who has disowned us."
Arthur Ernest Welch - retired, Ashford

Rachael was extremely helpful and was happy to answer as many questions as necessary to ensure that we fully understand the various documents. Very Professional, a pleasure to do Business with."
Jane Mitchell and Barry Dann - partners, Hawkhurst

" With a young family, a business, and never having had Wills before, we found the whole thing a minefield when researching the area. Then we met Rachael. She made the process clear for us, and was very professional and efficient in compiling our Wills. I thoroughly recommend Rachael as a Will writer - she gets our vote!"
Paul McLoughlin - Zuu Media, Sevenoaks

HTW
HEIR TIGHT WILLS

SPECIAL OFFER
FOR READERS
OF THIS BOOK

SPECIAL OFFER FOR READERS OF THIS BOOK

I hope this book has proven useful, and given you a better idea of how to make sure your family and your business are taken care of; both before and after you are gone.

Now that you understand why a properly prepared Will - along with Lasting Powers of Attorney and the right company documentation - are so important, let me explain how I can help you prepare yours.

Please read on for more information:

Free Consultation

To assist you in the implementation of your estate planning requirements, and as a *thank you* for reading this book, I'd like to offer you a *Free Telephone Consultation*, on any aspect of Wills and Estate Planning - at a time to suit you - followed up with a written report specific to your requirements.

To book your Free Consultation
call 0845 519 7585
or email your details to
info@heir-tight-wills.co.uk

Lightning Source UK Ltd.
Milton Keynes UK
UKOW051538290313

208391UK00007B/94/P